Table of Contents

Hi, friends! Today I'm talking to somebody very special. Her name is Wilma Rudolph. Wilma, would you tell us about yourself? We'd love to learn about your life.

Wilma says: Of course! In 1960, I became the first woman to win three gold medals in **track and field** in a single Olympics. After that, people called me the fastest woman on Earth. Black people didn't have the same rights as white people then. But when I came home from the Olympics, I was an American hero. My accomplishment was important to me for another reason too. You see, for much of my childhood, I couldn't walk. I had to work harder than other athletes to run well enough to win races.

CUB REPORTER

MEETS FAMOUS AMERICANS

WHAT'S YOUR STORY, WILMA RUDOLPH?

Krystyna Poray Goddu
illustrations by Doug Jones

Lerner Publications ◆ Minneapolis

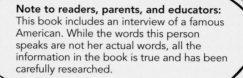

Note to readers, parents, and educators:
This book includes an interview of a famous American. While the words this person speaks are not her actual words, all the information in the book is true and has been carefully researched.

Lerner Publications Company
A division of Lerner Publishing Group, Inc.
241 First Avenue North
Minneapolis, MN 55401 USA

For reading levels and more information, look up this title at www.lernerbooks.com.

Main body text set in Avenir LT Pro 45 Book 15/21.
Typeface provided by Linotype AG.

Library of Congress Cataloging-in-Publication Data

Goddu, Krystyna Poray.
    What's your story, Wilma Rudolph? / Krystyna Poray Goddu.
        pages cm
    Includes bibliographical references and index.
    ISBN 978-1-4677-8782-6 (lb : alk. paper) — ISBN 978-1-4677-9643-9 (pb : alk. paper) — ISBN 978-1-4677-9644-6 (eb pdf)
    1. Rudolph, Wilma, 1940–1994—Juvenile literature. 2. Runners (Sports)—United States—Biography—Juvenile literature. 3. Women runners—United States—Biography—Juvenile literature. I. Title.
GV1061.15.R83G63 2016
796.42092—dc23 [B]   2015016195

Manufactured in the United States of America
1 – VP – 12/31/15

Wilma Rudolph shows off the three gold medals she won at the 1960 Olympic Games.

Where and when were you born?

Wilma says: I was born in a part of Clarksville, Tennessee, called Saint Bethlehem on June 23, 1940. I was number twenty of twenty-two children. My father had eleven children with his first wife. Then he had eleven more with my mother. I was a tiny baby. I weighed less than 5 pounds (2 kilograms) when I was born. It's hard to believe I grew to be nearly 6 feet (1.8 meters) tall!

Wilma *(right)*, aged six, poses for a photo with her older sister Yvonne. Wilma came from a large family with lots of siblings.

> Why weren't you able to walk when you were a child?

Wilma says: When I was four years old, I got very sick. I came down with three different illnesses. They are called pneumonia, scarlet fever, and polio. Many children died from polio back then. I was lucky enough to survive, but my left leg was **paralyzed**. That didn't stop me from getting around, though. I hopped on one foot everywhere I went. The school my brothers and sisters went to wouldn't let me attend because I couldn't walk. I cried every morning when I watched them leave for school.

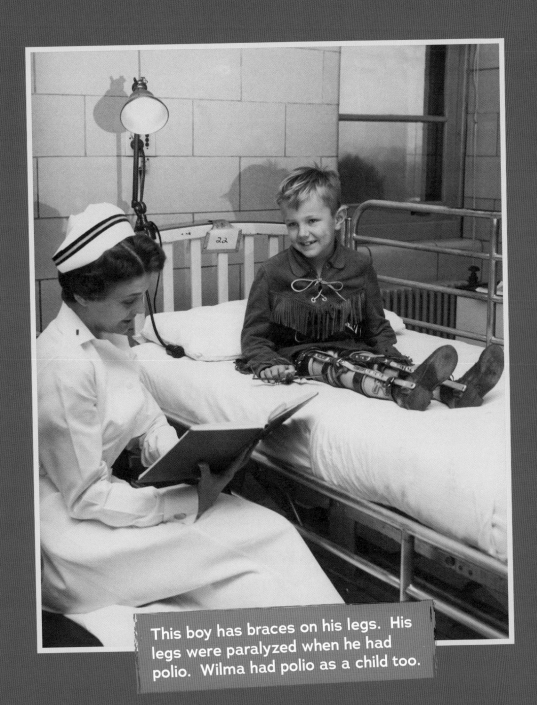

This boy has braces on his legs. His legs were paralyzed when he had polio. Wilma had polio as a child too.

How did you learn to walk again?

Wilma says: Every week, my mother and I boarded a bus and rode 45 miles (72 kilometers) to Nashville so I could have **physical therapy**. We had to sit in the back of the bus because buses were **segregated**. The law said only white people could sit in the front of buses.

When I was eight, I got a metal **brace** attached to a special shoe. That helped me start to take my first steps. Then I was allowed to go to school. When I was eleven, I was finally able to walk without the brace. One of the proudest moments of my childhood was the first time I walked down the aisle at the church my family went to.

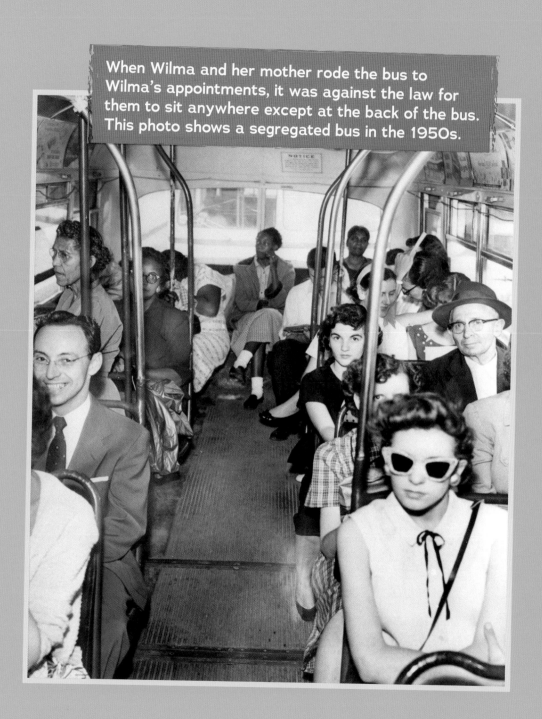

When Wilma and her mother rode the bus to Wilma's appointments, it was against the law for them to sit anywhere except at the back of the bus. This photo shows a segregated bus in the 1950s.

When did you begin to run?

Wilma says: I began to run when I was in high school. I also played basketball. I was a very good basketball player. My high school coach called me Skeeter. He said I was small and fast, just like a mosquito! When basketball season was finished, I ran in track events. I was a sprinter, or someone who runs short distances. I won lots of races. I was so fast that I impressed Ed Temple, the track coach at Tennessee State University. He wanted me to be on his team. It was called the Tigerbelles.

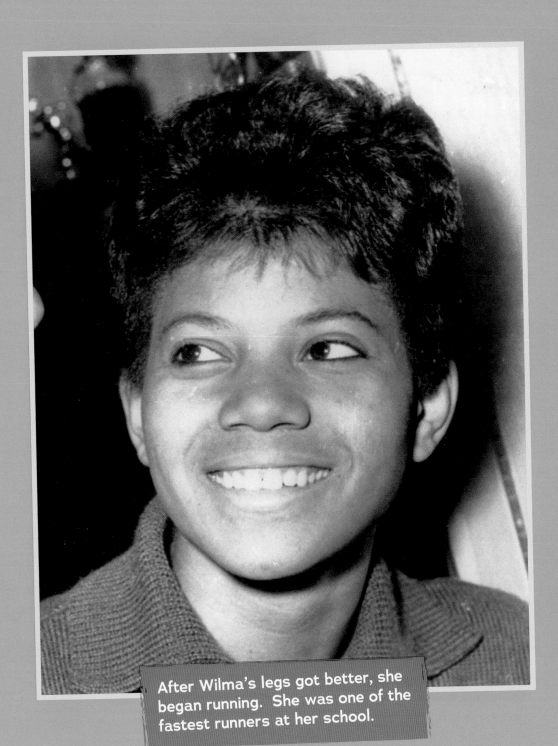

After Wilma's legs got better, she began running. She was one of the fastest runners at her school.

What was the first important race you won?

Wilma says: In 1955, I won both the 75-yard (69 m) dash and the 100-yard (91 m) dash at the **Amateur Athletic Union**. That gave me the courage to try out for the Olympics the next year. My Tigerbelle teammate Mae Faggs had already been in the Olympics twice. She and I both won spots on the US team in the 1956 Olympics in Melbourne, Australia. Two more Tigerbelles also made the US team. And Ed Temple became the coach of our Olympics team!

To win a spot in the Olympic 200-meter dash, runners first had to compete in the trials. Here Wilma *(left)* crosses the finish line just inches behind her US teammate Mae Faggs to make it into the finals!

Did you win any medals at the Olympics that year?

Wilma says: Yes, and I was so proud! I didn't run any races by myself, but I ran the 400-meter **relay** with the American team. We came in third place and earned a bronze medal. I loved the feeling of winning! I promised myself that at the next Olympics, I would win a medal on my own.

Wilma and her teammates won third place in the 400-meter relay. The 1956 US Olympic women's relay team included *(from left to right)* Margaret Matthews, Wilma, Mae Faggs, and Isabelle Daniels.

What was it like to go to the 1960 Olympics?

Wilma says: I was excited to represent the United States again. But I was nervous too. The Olympics were in Rome, Italy, and it was very hot there. Heat makes it harder to run. Also, many of the other runners were extremely fast. I knew it would be hard to beat them. And the Olympics were going to be on TV for the first time in history. Millions of people would be watching me!

As if these challenges weren't enough, something awful happened the day before the first race. I stepped into a hole on the practice track and twisted my ankle. Just walking was painful. Yet I was determined to run. I hadn't gone all the way to Rome to miss out on the Olympics!

Wilma springs out of the starting blocks in the 200-meter dash at the 1960 Summer Olympics in Rome.

What were the Olympics like for you after you got hurt?

Wilma says: They weren't easy. The doctors didn't think it was a good idea for me to compete. On the day of my first race, my ankle was still swollen and hurt a lot. But I ran anyway, and once I started, I forgot all about the pain. I focused on running as fast as I could. I ran the 100-meter dash in just over eleven seconds and won! Millions of people saw me earn my first Olympic gold medal on TV.

In front of thousands of fans, Wilma receives the Olympic gold medal for winning the 100-meter dash.

In what other events did you win gold medals?

Wilma says: I won my second gold medal for the 200-meter dash. The crowds in the stands were chanting my name. I ran in the rain, which made things extra tricky. Yet I still won. Then I ran the 400-meter relay with my team. As part of this race, I had to grab a **baton** from one of my teammates and run with it across the finish line. When I grabbed the baton, we were in first place. But then I almost dropped it! That slowed me down. We fell into third place. I knew we were behind, so I sped up as fast as I could. I made it to the finish line less than one second before anybody else.

Wilma *(second from left)* carries the baton across the finish line to help the 1960 US women's Olympic relay team win the gold medal.

Wilma and her teammates receive gold medals for their win in the 400-meter relay.

What happened when you came home from the Olympics?

Wilma says: The town of Clarksville, where I lived, held a big parade in my honor. It was going to be segregated, like parades were in most of the South. But I refused to be part of it if it was segregated. So it was decided that black people and white people could both attend the event after all. It was the first public event in Clarksville that wasn't segregated. I received other honors too. I was named Woman Athlete of the Year. President John F. Kennedy even invited me to the White House!

The town of Clarksville honored Wilma's achievements with a parade when she returned from Rome. Wilma insisted that both black people and white people be allowed to attend.

Did you keep running after you won the gold medals?

Wilma says: I **retired** from running in 1962. After that, I taught school and worked as a track coach. In 1967, I joined Operation Champ. This program organized a group of athletes who coached children and teenagers who didn't have anybody to teach them how to play sports. I loved sharing my story and my skills with them. In 1981, I started the Wilma Rudolph Foundation to help even more young people train in sports. It was important to me to give kids a chance to find and build their skills in athletics.

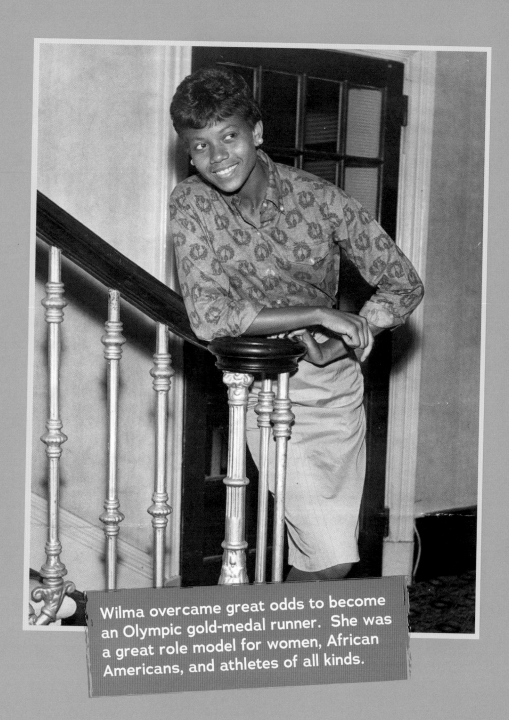

Wilma overcame great odds to become an Olympic gold-medal runner. She was a great role model for women, African Americans, and athletes of all kinds.

How did your achievements make a difference in the world?

Wilma says: My success as a strong female athlete has encouraged young women—and especially young black women—to be athletes too. I'm proud of that. But I'm even prouder that my life inspired all young people, black and white, to follow their dreams. My life shows that with determination and desire, you can overcome almost anything.

Timeline

1940   Wilma Glodean Rudolph is born in Tennessee.

1944   Wilma comes down with polio, which leaves her unable to walk.

1951   Wilma begins to walk on her own after years of physical therapy.

1955   Wilma wins the 75-yard (69 m) dash and the 100-yard (91 m) dash at the Amateur Athletic Union meet.

1956   Wilma wins a bronze medal in the Summer Olympic Games in Melbourne, Australia.

1960   Wilma becomes the first American woman to win three gold medals in track and field at the same Olympic Games. She also receives the Associated Press Woman Athlete of the Year award.

1962   Wilma retires from track.

1967   Wilma joins Operation Champ.

1981   Wilma creates the Wilma Rudolph Foundation.

1994   Wilma dies of brain cancer.

Glossary

Amateur Athletic Union: a group devoted to giving people of all ages the chance to play sports for fun

baton: a stick that is passed from one runner to another in a relay race

brace: a device that helps to support a part of the body

paralyzed: unable to move or feel anything

physical therapy: treatments designed to help an injured part of the body get better. Physical therapy can include heat, massage, and exercises.

relay: a sporting event in which team members take turns racing while competing against another team

retired: stopped working or playing a sport

segregated: separated based on race

track and field: the sport of running races

Further Information

Books

Berne, Emma Carlson. *What's Your Story, Jackie Robinson?* Minneapolis: Lerner Publications, 2016. Cub Reporter interviews another talented athlete who broke racial barriers.

Macceca, Stephanie. *Wilma Rudolph: Against All Odds.* Huntington Beach, CA: Teacher Created Materials, 2010. This book traces Wilma Rudolph's journey from her days as a child with polio to her victory in the Olympics.

Wade, Mary Dodson. *Amazing Olympic Athlete Wilma Rudolph.* Berkeley Heights, NJ: Enslow, 2010. Read more about Wilma's life both on the track and off.

Websites

ESPN: Wilma Rudolph
https://espn.go.com/sportscentury/features/00016444.html
This ESPN site includes many details about Wilma Rudolph's Olympics wins and what others had to say about her.

My Hero: Sports Hero Wilma Rudolph
http://myhero.com/hero.asp?hero=wilmarudolph
Find out why Wilma Rudolph is a hero to so many people.

Social Studies for Kids: Wilma Rudolph
http://www.socialstudiesforkids.com/articles/ushistory
/wilmarudolph.htm
Visit this website for a brief biography of Wilma.

Index

Photo Acknowledgments

The images in this book are used with the permission of: © Bettmann/CORBIS, pp. 5, 11, 19, 23 (top); Handout, p. 7; © Keystone-France/Gamma-Keystone/Getty Images, p. 9; AP Photo, pp. 13, 15, 17, 21, 23 (bottom); © George Silk/The LIFE Picture Collection/Getty Images, p. 25; Daily Mail/Rex//Rex USA, p. 27.

Front cover: © Angelo Cozzi; Mario De Biasi; Sergio Del Grande; Walter Mori/Mondadori Portfolio via Getty Images.